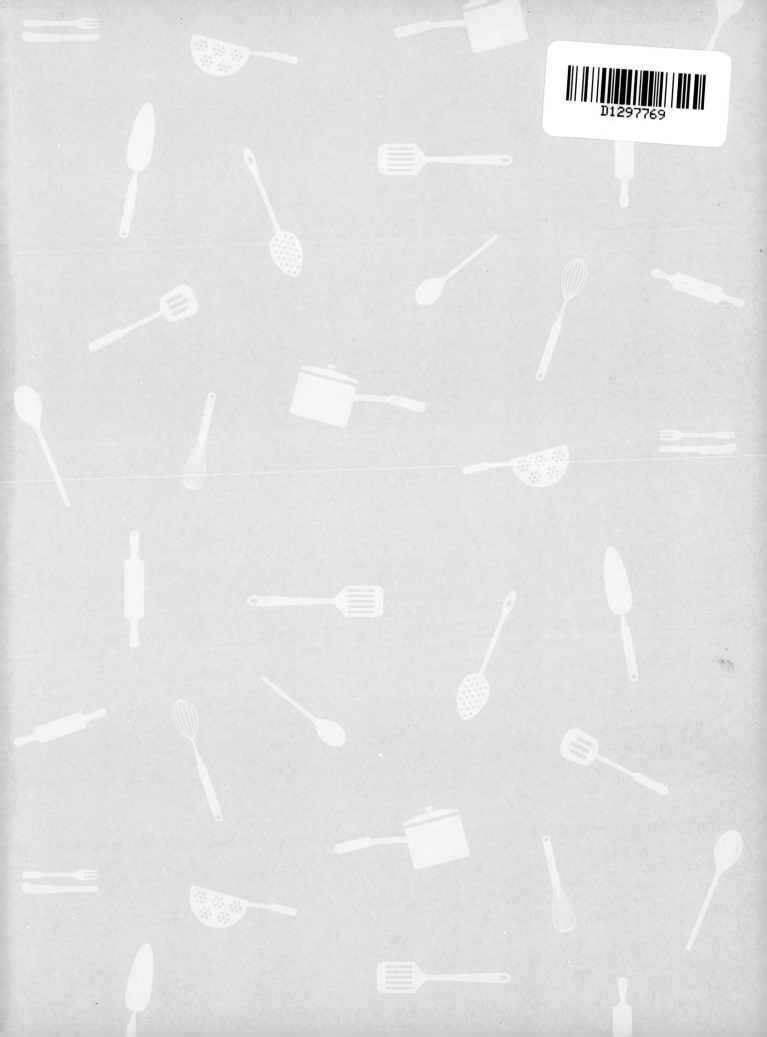

MAKE, BAKE AND CREATE
SWEET TREATS

BY NANCY LAMBERT

PUBLISHING PLC

Published by Top That! Publishing plc
Tide Mill Way, Woodbridge, Suffolk, IP12 1AP, UK
www.topthatpublishing.com

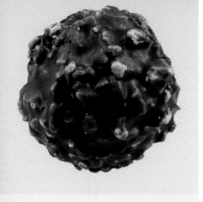

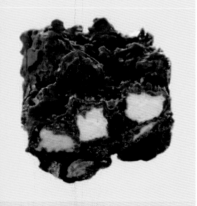

CONTENTS

Introduction	5
Equipment, Safety and Hygiene	7
Getting Started	9
Peanut Butter Cups	10
Chocolate Mice	11
Indoor Smores	12
Peppermint Creams	13
Nutty Nougat Parfait	14
Rock Candy	15
Lemon Poppy Muffins	16
Sticky Toffee Popcorn	17
Coconut Ice	18
Chocolate Drops	19
Caramel Lollipops	20
Chocolate Truffles	21
Honeycomb	22
Iced Biscuits	23
Vanilla Fudge	24
Peanut Brittle	25
Rocky Road	26
Flourless Brownies	27
Liquorice Truffles	28
Caramel Apples	29
Ice Cream Cones	30
Sweetie Cookies	31
Colourful Meringues	32
Chocolate Fondant Fancies	33
Traffic Light Jelly	34
Mini Jammy Tarts	35

Ice Cream Sandwiches **36**

Chocolate Bananas **37**

Caramel Shortcake **38**

Caramel Nut Sweets **39**

Brazilian Brigadeiro **40**

Hot Cross Buns **41**

Pumpkin Muffins **42**

Welsh Cakes **43**

Homemade Jaffa Cakes **44**

Fruity Lollies **45**

Cinnamon Buns **46**

Banana Walnut Muffins **47**

Doughnuts **48**

Macaroons **49**

Swedish Chocolate Balls **50**

Blueberry Muffins **51**

Blondies **52**

Scotch Pancakes **53**

Baklava **54**

Ladybird Biscuits **55**

Shortbread **56**

Crispy Cakes **57**

Scones **58**

Fruit Salad Sundaes **59**

Ice Cream Bon Bons **60**

Raspberry Semifreddo **61**

Date Muffins **62**

Chocolate Croissants **63**

Index of Recipes **64**

INTRODUCTION

Whether it's for a special occasion, such as a birthday or sleepover, or just for you and your family to enjoy, making sweet treats is always fun! If you're preparing treats for a specific occasion, remember to have everything organised in advance – work out what you are going to make beforehand and leave plenty of time so you don't feel rushed. If you can, make some of the food the day before and store it safely.

If you can, try and get your friends and family involved in the cooking. Why not invite your friends over to make all of your favourite recipes, then you can have a taste test afterwards! With such a wide variety of sweet treats included, you're sure to find something to suit every occasion, from an after-school snack to a midnight feast!

This book will provide you with a selection of delicious sweet recipes for adults and junior chefs to make together. And remember, once you have perfected the recipes, don't be afraid to experiment with the ingredients, flavours and toppings to create and decorate your very own sweet treats!

COOKING TIPS!

- Make sure you use the freshest ingredients available.

- If you're using dark chocolate in a recipe, look for good-quality dark chocolate with about 70% cocoa solids for the best flavour.

- Remember, you can adapt any recipe to suit your specific tastes, for example leave nuts out of recipes or replace them with a dried fruit.

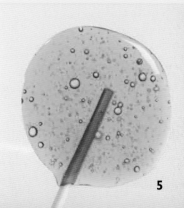

EQUIPMENT

- To complete the recipes in this book, you will need to use a selection of everyday cooking equipment and utensils, such as mixing bowls, saucepans, a sieve, knives, spoons and forks and a chopping board.

- Of course, you'll need to weigh and measure the ingredients, so you'll need a measuring jug and some kitchen scales too.

- To make some of the recipes in this book, you'll need to use special kitchen equipment. These items (and others that you may not have to hand) are listed at the start of each recipe.

SAFETY & HYGIENE

- Before starting any cooking always wash your hands.

- Cover any cuts with a plaster.

- Wear an apron to protect your clothes.

- Always make sure that all the equipment you use is clean.

- If you need to use a sharp knife to cut up something hard, ask an adult to help you. Always use a chopping board.

- Remember that trays in the oven and pans on the cooker can get very hot. Always ask an adult to turn on the oven and to get things in and out of the oven for you.

- Always ask an adult for help if you are using anything electrical – like an electric whisk.

- Be careful when heating anything in a pan on top of the cooker. Keep the handle turned to one side to avoid accidentally knocking the pan.

- Keep your pets out of the kitchen while cooking.

GETTING STARTED

MEASURING

Use scales to weigh exactly how much of each ingredient you need or use a measuring jug to measure liquids.

MIXING

Use a spoon, balloon whisk or electric hand whisk to mix the ingredients together.

CREATING RECIPES

Once you've made a recipe in this book a few times, think about whether you could make your own version. Don't be afraid to experiment with the recipes to find something you like. Try to think up names for the things you create!

PLEASE NOTE

The temperatures and measurements given in this book are approximate. Use the same measurement conversions throughout your recipe (grams or ounces) to maintain the correct ratios. All of the recipes in this book have been created for adults to make with junior chefs and must not be attempted by an unsupervised child.

Read through each recipe to make sure you've got all the ingredients that you need before you start.

PEANUT BUTTER CUPS

Extra equipment:
- microwaveable bowl
- mini paper cases

Ingredients:
- 60 g (2 oz) smooth peanut butter
- 15 g (½ oz) butter
- pinch of salt
- 25 g (1 oz) icing sugar
- 250 g (9 oz) dark chocolate
- 5 g (¼ oz) butter

1 Put the peanut butter, butter and salt in a microwaveable bowl and heat in the microwave for about one minute or until just soft, but not melted (check and stir the ingredients every 20 seconds).

2 Stir in the icing sugar.

3 Ask an adult to melt the chocolate and 5 g (¼ oz) butter in a heatproof bowl placed over a saucepan of simmering water, making sure the bowl doesn't touch the water.

4 Drop a teaspoon of the melted chocolate into each of the mini paper cases, just enough to cover the base.

5 Place a small amount of the peanut butter mixture in the centre of the chocolate base. Then, cover with more melted chocolate, enough to fully cover the peanut butter mixture, top and sides.

6 Place the peanut butter cups in the refrigerator until set.

TOP TIP!
White and milk chocolate are great variations of this recipe!

CHOCOLATE MICE

Extra equipment:
- baking tray
- baking paper

Ingredients:
- 100 g (3 ½ oz) dark chocolate
- 12 glacé cherries with stalks
- 12 mini meringues
- flaked almonds
- 1 tube white writing icing
- 1 tube black writing icing

1 Line the baking tray with baking paper.

2 Ask an adult to put a heatproof bowl over a pan of simmering water, making sure the bowl doesn't touch the water.

3 Put the dark chocolate in the bowl and stir until melted. Ask an adult to take the bowl off the heat.

4 Then, dip each cherry into the chocolate using the stalk. Repeat with the mini meringues, making sure each is thoroughly coated in chocolate.

5 While the chocolate is still soft, press two flaked almonds onto the cherry to look like ears, then sandwich them between the cherry and the meringue.

6 Repeat and then leave each mouse on the baking tray to set.

7 Finally, use the white writing icing to give each mouse eyes. Finish with dots of black icing.

TOP TIP!
If you don't have any writing icing use white chocolate buttons for the eyes.

11

INDOOR SMORES

Extra equipment:
- 20 cm (8 in.) cake tin
- baking paper

Ingredients:
- 150 g (5 ½ oz) digestive biscuits, broken into crumbs
- 50 g (1 ¾ oz) oats
- 25 g (1 oz) granulated sugar
- 100 g (3 ½ oz) butter, melted
- 170 g (6 oz) dark chocolate, broken into chunks
- 130 g (4 ½ oz) mini marshmallows

1 Preheat the oven to 180°C / 350°F / gas mark 4. Line the base and sides of the cake tin with baking paper.

2 Mix the digestive crumbs and oats with the sugar. Then, add the melted butter and stir together until the crumbs are covered. Press about half the mixture into the bottom of the cake tin and bake in the oven for about 10 minutes, or until the crust turns golden brown.

3 Ask an adult to remove from the oven and evenly sprinkle the chocolate over the base. Then, sprinkle the marshmallows on top and cover with the remaining crumble mixture.

4 Put the mixture back in the oven and bake for another 10 minutes, or until the marshmallows and chocolate are beginning to melt.

5 Once completely cool, lift from the tin using the baking paper.

6 Cut into slices and enjoy!

TOP TIP!
Smores are an American bonfire classic. You can replace the dark chocolate with white or milk chocolate if you prefer.

PEPPERMINT CREAMS

SERVES 8

Extra equipment:

- whisk
- rolling pin
- small round cookie cutter
- baking tray

Ingredients:

- 1 egg white
- 1/2 lemon, juice only
- 1 teaspoon peppermint flavouring
- 425 g (15 oz) icing sugar
- green and pink food colouring (optional)

1 Whisk the egg white in a bowl until it forms stiff peaks. Slowly whisk in the lemon juice, peppermint flavouring and icing sugar until you have a stiff paste.

2 Divide the mixture into three equal parts. If desired, add a few drops of green food colouring to one part of the paste, until it is the colour wanted, and mix well. Repeat with the pink food colouring.

3 Place each mixture onto a work surface, dust with icing sugar and roll each out to about 1 cm (1/2 in.) thick.

4 Cut out small circles from each mixture using a cookie cutter and place onto the baking tray.

5 Put the peppermint creams in the refrigerator for 1–2 hours, or until the mixture has set.

TOP TIP!
Try coating your peppermint creams in 150 g (6 oz) melted dark chocolate.

NUTTY NOUGAT PARFAIT

SERVES 6

Extra equipment:
- 450 g (1 lb) loaf tin
- baking tray
- greaseproof paper
- cling film
- rolling pin
- whisk

Ingredients:
- butter, for greasing
- 190 g (7 oz) caster sugar
- 50 g (2 oz) walnuts, chopped
- 4 egg whites
- 190 ml (6 1/2 fl.oz) double cream, lightly whipped

1 Grease the loaf tin with the butter.

2 Ask an adult to heat 125 g (4 1/2 oz) of the sugar in a pan over a low heat until it melts and becomes sticky and golden-brown.

3 Stir in the walnuts, then pour the mixture onto a baking tray lined with greaseproof paper. Leave the mixture to set.

4 Once set, cover with cling film and break into pieces using a rolling pin. Set aside.

5 Whisk the egg whites in a bowl until they form soft peaks. Gradually add the remaining 65 g (2 1/2 oz) of sugar, whisking continuously until it forms stiff peaks.

6 With a metal spoon, mix in the cream and sugared nut pieces until well combined.

7 Pour the nougat parfait mixture into the greased loaf tin and place in the freezer until completely frozen.

8 To serve, turn out the nougat parfait onto a plate and cut into slices.

TOP TIP!
Try serving with chopped fresh fruit or a fruit purée.

ROCK CANDY

Extra equipment:
- cotton string, cut to 3/4 depth of each jar, or four wooden skewers
- 4 pencils (to suspend the string in the jar)
- greaseproof paper
- 4 clean glass jars

Ingredients:
- 1 litre (1 3/4 pints) water
- 900 g (2 lb) granulated sugar
- a few drops food colouring (you can choose any colour you like)

1 Ask an adult to heat the water in a saucepan over a medium heat until it comes to the boil.

2 Then ask an adult to put the sugar in the boiling water, a little at a time, and stir continuously until the sugar has dissolved completely and the water is clear.

3 Add 1–2 teaspoons of food colouring and stir until the colour is even. Then, ask an adult to take the saucepan off the heat and leave to cool for about 10 minutes.

4 Tie one end of each string to the pencils and then ask an adult to carefully dip each string into the sugar syrup. Alternatively, dip the wooden skewers into the sugar syrup. Remove from the syrup and lay on a piece of greaseproof paper.

5 Once cooled, pour the sugar syrup equally into the jars. Then, carefully lower one sugared string or skewer into each jar until they are about 2 1/2 cm (1 in.) from the bottom.

6 Cover the top of the jars with greaseproof paper and place them away from harsh lights where they can sit at room temperature, undisturbed.

7 Don't touch or move the jars as it will disturb the crystals forming. Leave for about seven days and then carefully remove the rock candy from the jar. Leave to dry for a few minutes and then enjoy!

LEMON POPPY MUFFINS

MAKES 12

Extra equipment:
- paper cases
- muffin baking tray

Ingredients:
- 375 g (13 oz) plain flour
- 1 tablespoon baking powder
- 1/2 teaspoon bicarbonate of soda
- 2 tablespoons poppy seeds
- 140 g (5 oz) unsalted butter
- 200 g (7 oz) sugar
- 2 eggs
- 1 tablespoon lemon zest
- 350 ml (12 fl.oz) plain yogurt

For the topping:
- 2 tablespoons fresh lemon juice
- 120 g (4 oz) icing sugar

1 Preheat the oven to 190°C / 375°F / gas mark 5. Put the paper cases in the muffin baking tray.

2 Ask an adult to help you grate the lemon, but be careful not to grate any of the white pith. Cut the lemon in half and squeeze the juice into a bowl and set aside.

3 Mix together the flour, baking powder, bicarbonate of soda and poppy seeds, and set aside.

4 In a large mixing bowl, cream the butter and sugar together, beating until fluffy. Beat in the eggs one at a time. Add the lemon zest and then beat in half of the dry ingredients and half of the yogurt.

5 Next, beat in the remaining dry ingredients followed by the remaining yogurt.

6 Spoon the mixture into the paper cases, and bake the muffins for 25–30 minutes, or until they are golden brown.

7 For the icing, put the icing sugar into a bowl with the lemon juice. Mix together well, until it forms a smooth paste.

8 While the muffins are still warm, spoon a little of the icing over each one. Leave to cool completely.

STICKY TOFFEE POPCORN

Ingredients:

- 2 tablespoons sunflower oil
- 100 g (4 oz) popping corn
- 25 g (1 oz) butter

For the toffee:

- 50 g (2 oz) butter
- 50 g (2 oz) brown sugar
- 2 tablespoons golden syrup
- pinch of salt

1 Ask an adult to heat the oil in a large saucepan and sprinkle in the popping corn, making sure that it is coated evenly in oil.

2 Next, cover with a lid, turn the heat down, and listen for popping noises. As soon as the popping quietens down, take the pan off the heat.

3 Next, make the toffee sauce – melt the butter, add the brown sugar and golden syrup to a pan and stir over a high heat for 1–2 minutes.

4 For plain popcorn, tip half of the popcorn out of the saucepan and into a bowl. Toss with 25 g (1 oz) of butter and a pinch of salt.

5 For toffee popcorn, pour the toffee sauce over the remaining popcorn, replace the lid on the pan and shake to mix together well.

6 Pour out into a bowl and serve when cooled!

COCONUT ICE

MAKES 36

Extra equipment:
- 18 cm (7 in.) square baking tin
- greaseproof paper

Ingredients:
- 225 g (8 oz) icing sugar
- 25 g (1 oz) butter
- 150 ml (5 fl.oz) sweetened condensed milk
- 225 g (8 oz) desiccated coconut
- pink food colouring

1 Put the tin on the greaseproof paper, and draw around it. Cut out the square so that it is large enough to overlap the sides. Then, slit the corners and put the paper into the tin.

2 Ask an adult to help you put the icing sugar, butter and sweetened condensed milk into a pan over a medium heat, and bring the mixture to the boil. Let the mixture simmer for 4 minutes, stirring all the time.

3 Remove the pan from the heat and stir in the coconut.

4 Ask an adult to pour half of the mixture into the tin. Leave it to cool and set.

5 Colour the other half of the mixture with a few drops of food colouring. Pour it on top of the mixture in the tin, and leave it to set.

6 Cut the coconut ice into slices, but be careful – it will be very crumbly!

CHOCOLATE DROPS

Extra equipment:
- baking tray
- greaseproof paper

Ingredients:
- 200 g (7 oz) chocolate (white, milk or dark)
- 30 g (1 oz) walnuts
- 30 g (1 oz) almonds
- 30 g (1 oz) dried fruit

1 Line the baking tray with greaseproof paper.

2 Ask an adult to melt the chocolate in a heatproof bowl over a pan of simmering water, making sure the base of the bowl doesn't touch the water.

3 Use a tablespoon to spoon the melted chocolate onto the greaseproof paper to form discs.

4 Sprinkle the walnuts, almonds and dried fruit evenly over the melted chocolate drops.

5 Place the chocolate drops in the refrigerator to set.

6 Once set, peel the chocolate drops off the greaseproof paper and enjoy!

TOP TIP!
Experiment with different toppings – why not try your favourite sweets?

CARAMEL LOLLIPOPS

Extra equipment:
- baking tray
- baking paper
- 8 wooden lollipop sticks

Ingredients:
- 150 g (5 1/4 oz) golden granulated sugar
- sea salt flakes

1 Line the baking tray with baking paper and place the tray onto a heatproof surface as the caramel will get very hot.

2 Pour the sugar into a large metal saucepan (don't use a black non-stick pan) so you will be able to judge the colour of the caramel.

3 Ask an adult to put the pan on a low heat and wait for the sugar to melt and begin to change colour. If one area begins to colour more quickly, swirl the pan around to even it out.

4 Leave the sugar to caramelise until it has reached a dark golden colour. Then, add a few sea salt flakes and swirl them around the caramel.

5 Ask an adult to carefully pour rounds of the caramel onto the baking paper and quickly stick a lollipop stick in each.

6 Leave to cool completely.

TOP TIP!
Wrap your lollipops in plastic cellophane, tie with a ribbon and give them as a gift!

20

CHOCOLATE TRUFFLES

Extra equipment:
- plastic container

Ingredients:
- 150 g (6 oz) plain chocolate
- 150 ml (5 fl.oz) double cream
- 25 g (1 oz) butter
- cocoa powder, to dust

1 Ask an adult to put a heatproof bowl over a saucepan of simmering water, making sure the bowl doesn't touch the water.

2 Break the chocolate into small pieces and put it in the bowl, then add the cream and butter. Stir the mixture until the chocolate has melted.

3 Take the saucepan off the heat. Take the bowl off the saucepan and leave it to cool for a few minutes.

4 Carefully pour the melted chocolate into the plastic container. Put the lid on the container and leave it in the refrigerator for 3–4 hours.

5 Remove the container from the refrigerator and roll small balls of the chocolate truffle mixture in your hands. Try not to hold the mixture for too long as it will start to melt.

6 Roll each ball in cocoa powder until well coated.

7 Store the truffles in a container in the refrigerator until you are ready to eat them.

TOP TIP!
Try coating the truffles in chopped nuts or desiccated coconut.

21

HONEYCOMB

Extra equipment:
- 18 cm (7 in.) square baking tin
- wooden spoon

Ingredients:
- butter, for greasing
- 5 tablespoons caster sugar
- 2 tablespoons golden syrup
- 1 teaspoon bicarbonate of soda

1 Use a paper towel to grease the baking tin with a little butter.

2 Ask an adult to help you put the sugar and syrup into a saucepan over a medium heat. Bring the mixture to the boil and then let it simmer for about 3–4 minutes until it becomes golden brown.

3 Take the pan off the heat, add the bicarbonate of soda and mix it in with a wooden spoon. As soon as the mixture froths up, pour it into the baking tin.

4 When the mixture has cooled, turn it out onto a chopping board and use a wooden spoon to crack it into bite-sized pieces.

TOP TIP!
Crushed up pieces of honeycomb taste great sprinkled over ice cream.

ICED BISCUITS

Extra equipment:
• baking tray
• baking paper
• sieve
• rolling pin
• cookie cutters
• palette knife

Ingredients:
• 100 g (4 oz) butter
• 100 g (4 oz) caster sugar
• 1 egg
• 1 teaspoon vanilla extract
• 275 g (10 oz) plain flour

For the icing:
• 400 g (14 oz) icing sugar
• 3–4 tablespoons water
• food colouring (optional)
• assorted sugar sprinkles, sweets, edible glitter (optional)

1 Preheat the oven to 190°C / 375°F / gas mark 5. Line the baking tray with baking paper.

2 Cream the butter and sugar together in a bowl until light and fluffy. Add the egg and vanilla extract, a little at a time, and mix well.

3 Sift the flour into the creamed mixture and, using your hands, create a smooth, firm dough. Refrigerate the mixture for 15 minutes.

4 Roll the dough out on a floured surface until it is 1 cm (1/2 in.) thick. Using either a sharp knife or cookie cutters, cut out shapes from the dough and transfer to the baking tray.

5 Bake the cookies in the oven for 8–10 minutes, or until golden brown, then transfer to a wire rack to cool.

6 To make the icing, sift the icing sugar into a bowl and add enough water to make a smooth, thick paste. Add one or two drops of food colouring if you wish.

7 Use the palette knife to spread the icing over the cookies and leave to set. Top with sugar sprinkles, sweets or edible glitter.

TOP TIP!
Separate the icing into batches and add different food colouring to each for rainbow-coloured biscuits!

VANILLA FUDGE

MAKES 36

Extra equipment:
- 18 cm (7 in.) square cake tin
- sugar thermometer

Ingredients:
- 300 ml (10 fl.oz) milk
- 350 g (12 1/4 oz) caster sugar
- 100 g (4 oz) butter
- 1 teaspoon vanilla extract
- 75 g (2 1/2 oz) glacé cherries

1 Grease the cake tin with a little oil.

2 Ask an adult to put the milk, sugar and butter in a heavy-based saucepan. Gradually heat, stirring all the time, until the sugar has dissolved and the butter has melted.

3 Ask an adult to bring the mixture to the boil. Boil for 15–20 minutes, stirring all the time.

4 Put the sugar thermometer into the mixture and watch carefully until it reaches 115°C / 239°F (the soft-ball stage). Then, remove from the heat and stir in the vanilla extract. Leave to cool for 5 minutes.

5 Beat the mixture with a spoon for a few minutes until it begins to thicken and the gloss disappears. Stir in the glacé cherries.

6 Ask an adult to pour the mixture into the tin and leave to set at room temperature. Don't place the mixture in the refrigerator.

7 Once set, cut the fudge into small squares. Store in an airtight container.

PEANUT BRITTLE

Extra equipment:
- baking tray
- tin foil
- wooden spoon

Ingredients:
- 200 g (8 oz) caster sugar
- 60 ml (2 1/4 fl.oz) water
- 150 g (5 1/2 oz) golden syrup
- 150 g (5 1/2 oz) salted peanuts
- 1 1/2 teaspoons vanilla extract
- 25 g (1 oz) butter, softened
- 1 1/4 teaspoons bicarbonate of soda

1 Line the baking tray with tin foil and then grease well with butter. Place it by the cooker, ready for the hot brittle.

2 Ask an adult to put the sugar, water and syrup into a metal pan. Heat the mixture until it is gently boiling and then turn up the heat and boil for 5 minutes. The mixture should turn a deep amber colour. It may take more than 5 minutes and smoke a little before it's ready, but watch the colour carefully.

3 Ask an adult to take the pan off the heat and, with a wooden spoon, stir in the peanuts, followed by the vanilla extract, butter and bicarbonate of soda. The mixture should turn golden and frothy.

4 Carefully pour this onto the lined baking tray and use the wooden spoon to level out the mixture. Be careful as the mixture will be extremely hot.

5 Leave the brittle to cool completely and then break into pieces using a wooden spoon or rolling pin. Store in an airtight container to keep fresh.

TOP TIP!
Take extra care when heating the sugar to make sure it doesn't burn.

ROCKY ROAD

Extra equipment:
- 23 cm (9 in.) square baking tin
- clean freezer bag
- rolling pin
- spatula

Ingredients:
- 125 g (4 ¹/₂ oz) butter, softened
- 300 g (10 ¹/₂ oz) dark chocolate, broken into pieces
- 45 ml (1 ¹/₂ fl.oz) golden syrup
- 200 g (7 oz) digestive biscuits
- 100 g (3 ¹/₂ oz) mini marshmallows
- 50 g (1 ³/₄ oz) dried cranberries
- 50 g (1 ³/₄ oz) toasted pistachios, chopped
- 50 g (1 ³/₄ oz) milk chocolate chunks

1 Grease the baking tin with a little butter. Ask an adult to melt the butter, chocolate and golden syrup in a saucepan. When melted, mix well.

2 Put the biscuits into a freezer bag and break up with a rolling pin until you have a mixture of fine crumbs and small pieces.

3 Mix the biscuit pieces into the melted chocolate mixture in the saucepan. Then add the marshmallows, cranberries and chopped pistachios.

4 Tip into the baking tin and flatten with a spatula. Sprinkle the milk chocolate chunks over the top.

5 Refrigerate for about 2 hours, or preferably overnight.

6 To serve, cut into 25 squares. Keep refrigerated.

TOP TIP!
If you don't like marshmallows, add 100 g (3 ¹/₂ oz) raisins in step 3.

FLOURLESS BROWNIES

Extra equipment:
- 23 cm (9 in.) square baking tin
- baking paper

Ingredients:
- 225 g (8 oz) dark chocolate
- 225 g (8 oz) butter
- 2 teaspoons vanilla extract
- 200 g (7 oz) caster sugar
- 3 eggs, beaten
- 150 g (5 1/4 oz) ground almonds
- 100 g (3 1/2 oz) walnuts, chopped

1 Preheat the oven to 170°C / 340°F / gas mark 3. Line the baking tin with baking paper.

2 Ask an adult to slowly melt the dark chocolate and butter in a heavy-based saucepan.

3 Take the pan off the heat, mix in the vanilla extract and sugar and then let the mixture cool a bit.

4 In a separate bowl beat the eggs and then add to the chocolate mixture. Then, mix in the ground almonds and chopped walnuts. Pour the mixture into the baking tin and smooth the top.

5 Ask an adult to place the baking tin in the oven and bake for 25–30 minutes. The brownie should be cooked on top, but still soft underneath.

6 Once cool, remove from the tin and cut into squares.

TOP TIP!
Warm brownies taste great with vanilla ice cream.

LIQUORICE TRUFFLES

SERVES 6

Ingredients:
- 110 ml (4 fl.oz) double cream
- 15 g (½ oz) butter
- 110 g (4 oz) dark chocolate, finely chopped
- 75 g (3 oz) sweetened liquorice, finely chopped
- cocoa powder, to dust

1 Ask an adult to put the cream and butter into a saucepan and bring to the boil. Add the dark chocolate and stir until completely melted and smooth.

2 Remove from the heat and stir in the finely chopped liquorice. Then, put the mixture into a bowl and allow to cool. Place in the refrigerator to chill.

3 When the mixture is cold and has set, take teaspoonfuls and form into small balls with your hands.

4 Roll each truffle in cocoa powder and serve.

TOP TIP!
These truffles make great gifts – wrap them in a fancy box tied with ribbon to give to your friends!

CARAMEL APPLES

Extra equipment:
- baking tray
- baking paper
- 6 wooden sticks

Ingredients:
- 6 small apples
- 225 g (8 oz) granulated sugar
- 110 ml (4 fl.oz) water
- 30 g (1 oz) butter
- 2 tablespoons golden syrup
- 4 tablespoons mixed nuts, finely chopped (optional)

1 Line the baking tray with baking paper.

2 Push the wooden sticks halfway into each apple at the stalk end.

3 Ask an adult to dissolve the sugar and water in a thick-bottomed pan over a gentle heat.

4 Add the butter and syrup to the mixture and ask an adult to bring to the boil. Reduce the heat and simmer for 12–15 minutes, or until the caramel is a deep, amber colour. Don't stir the caramel at this stage or it will become grainy.

5 Remove the pan from the heat and allow to cool slightly.

6 Carefully dip each apple into the caramel, making sure it is well coated, then place on the baking tray to cool and harden. Dip the apples into the chopped nuts before allowing to cool completely (optional).

TOP TIP!
Experiment with the toppings – try melted chocolate instead!

ICE CREAM CONES

Extra equipment:

• electric whisk

• ice cream maker (optional)

• ice cream scoop (optional)

Ingredients:

• 500 ml (17 fl.oz) double cream

• 1 vanilla pod, split

• 100 g (4 oz) caster sugar

• 150 ml (5 fl.oz) water

• 4 egg yolks

• wafer cones, to serve

1 Ask an adult to heat the cream in a saucepan so that it almost boils and then remove from the heat. Add the split vanilla pod and leave it until the cream is completely cool.

2 Scrape the tiny seeds from the vanilla pod into the cream and remove the pod casing.

3 Dissolve the sugar in the water over a low heat. Then, ask an adult to turn up the heat and boil the mixture to create a light syrup. Leave the syrup mixture to cool for 1 minute.

4 Place the egg yolks in a bowl and ask an adult to whisk them using an electric whisk, slowly adding the hot syrup.

5 Continue to whisk until the mixture thickens and is mousse-like. Then, whisk in the cream and pour into an ice cream maker and churn until frozen. Alternatively, if you don't have an ice cream maker you can freeze your ice cream in a plastic tub in the freezer. You will need to stir the mixture every hour to break up any ice.

6 Serve your ice cream in ice cream cones for a special treat!

TOP TIP!
Make chocolate or strawberry ice cream by adding 300 g (10 oz) melted chocolate or 350 g (12 oz) puréed fresh strawberries when you whisk in the cream.

SWEETIE COOKIES

Extra equipment:

- baking tray
- baking paper
- rolling pin
- shaped cookie cutters

Ingredients:

- 125 g (4 oz) butter, softened
- 175 g (6 oz) caster sugar
- 1 egg
- 1 tablespoon golden syrup
- 250 g (9 oz) plain flour
- 1/2 teaspoon baking powder
- 2 teaspoons ground ginger

To decorate:

- icing sugar, for dusting
- assorted sweets

1 Preheat the oven to 180°C / 350°F / gas mark 4. Line the baking tray with baking paper.

2 Cream the butter and sugar together in a bowl until light and fluffy.

3 Lightly beat the egg and stir into the butter mixture with the golden syrup.

4 Mix in the flour, baking powder and ground ginger. Stir until well combined.

5 Roll out the mixture until it is about 1/2 cm (1/4 in.) thick. Use the cookie cutters to cut out the cookies then place onto the baking tray. Re-roll any leftover mixture and cut again.

6 Ask an adult to place the cookies into the oven and bake for 8–10 minutes, or until golden-brown.

7 Lay out on a wire rack and dust generously with icing sugar while the cookies are still warm, so the icing sugar will melt. To finish, decorate the cookies with your favourite sweets before the icing sugar sets.

COLOURFUL MERINGUES

Extra equipment:
- 2 baking trays
- baking paper
- large glass mixing bowl
- electric whisk
- sieve
- large metal spoon
- piping bag

Ingredients:
- 4 large eggs, whites only
- 115 g (4 oz) caster sugar
- 115 g (4 oz) icing sugar
- food colouring (optional)

1 Preheat the oven to 110°C / 230°F / gas mark 1/4. Line both baking trays with baking paper.

2 Pour the egg whites into a large, clean glass mixing bowl. Ask an adult to beat them with an electric whisk until the mixture holds stiff peaks. Alternatively, use a hand whisk – you'll just have to work extra hard!

3 Continue whisking then gradually add the caster sugar, a dessertspoonful at a time. Continue beating and adding the caster sugar. When ready, the mixture should be thick and glossy.

4 Sift a third of the icing sugar into the mixture, then gently fold it in using a large metal spoon.

5 Continue to sift and fold in the icing sugar a third at a time. Add a few drops of food colouring, if desired. Be careful not to over-mix the meringue.

6 Place the mixture into a piping bag and squeeze 3.5 cm (1 1/2 in.) 'blobs' of the mixture onto the baking trays and ask an adult to quickly place them into the oven for 1 1/4 hours, until the meringues sound crisp when tapped underneath.

7 Remove from the baking trays and leave to cool on a wire rack.

TOP TIP! Try sandwiching two meringues together with whipped double cream!

CHOCOLATE FONDANT FANCIES

Extra equipment:

- 23 cm (9 in.) square baking tin
- baking paper
- whisk

Ingredients:

- 175 g (6 oz) unsalted butter, plus extra for greasing
- 150 g (5 1/2 oz) caster sugar
- 3 eggs
- 175 g (6 oz) plain flour
- 1 teaspoon baking powder

For the icing:

- 25 g (1 oz) unsalted butter
- 90 g (3 oz) icing sugar, sifted
- 50 g (1 3/4 oz) dark chocolate
- 50 g (1 3/4 oz) white chocolate
- 100 ml (3 1/2 fl.oz) boiling water
- 75 g (2 1/2 oz) mascarpone
- red writing icing, to decorate

1 Preheat the oven to 140°C / 280°F / gas mark 1. Line the baking tin.

2 Whisk the butter and sugar together in a large bowl until pale and fluffy. Gradually add the eggs, whisking continuously. Then, carefully mix in the flour and baking powder until well combined.

3 Spoon the cake batter into the baking tin and bake for 25–30 minutes, until risen and golden. Set aside to cool, then cut into squares.

4 For the icing, ask an adult to put a heatproof bowl over a pan of simmering water, making sure the bowl doesn't touch the water. In one bowl, mix 15 g (1/2 oz) butter, 45 g (1 1/2 oz) icing sugar and the dark chocolate and stir until glossy and smooth. Gradually add some boiling water until the mixture is loose and slightly runny. Repeat in a separate bowl using the white chocolate and remaining butter and icing sugar.

5 Decorate each cake square with a teaspoon of mascarpone and smooth over the top. Then, spoon over enough of the dark icing to cover half of the cake squares. Repeat with the white icing. Set aside for 20–30 minutes, or until the icing has set.

6 Once cool, carefully drizzle some red writing icing over the iced fondant fancies.

TRAFFIC LIGHT JELLY

Extra equipment:
- heatproof jug
- 3 small dishes
- whisk
- 4 sundae glasses

Ingredients:
- 135 g (5 oz) lime jelly
- 135 g (5 oz) strawberry jelly
- 135 g (5 oz) orange jelly
- 300 ml (10 fl.oz) double cream
- chocolate strands, to serve

1 Cut the lime jelly into cubes and put it into a heatproof jug. Ask an adult to prepare the jelly, following the packet instructions. Stir the jelly with a wooden spoon until it has all dissolved. Pour the jelly into one of the small dishes and place in the refrigerator to set.

2 Make the strawberry and orange jellies, as above.

3 Once the jelly has set, whip the cream until it forms stiff peaks.

4 Spoon a quarter of the lime jelly into each sundae glass. Then, spoon some whipped cream on top.

5 Next, spoon a quarter of the strawberry jelly in each glass, top with cream and then finally add the orange jelly.

6 Top with a small spoonful of whipped cream and sprinkle with chocolate strands to serve.

TOP TIP! Decorate your jelly sundaes with fruit and mint leaves.

MINI JAMMY TARTS

Extra equipment:
• tart tray
• cookie cutters

Ingredients:
• butter, for greasing
• 250 g (9 oz) ready-made sweet shortcrust pastry
• plain flour, for dusting

For the filling:
• 450 g (1 lb) strawberries, hulls removed
• 450 g (1 lb) golden caster sugar
• 1 tablespoon vanilla extract
• mint leaves, to serve

1 Preheat the oven to 180°C / 350°F / gas mark 4. Grease the tart tray with butter.

2 On a lightly floured surface, roll out the shortcrust pastry to 1/2 cm (1/4 in.).

3 Use a cookie cutter to cut discs from the pastry that are slightly bigger than the holes in the tart tray. Press a pastry disc into each of the holes.

4 Put the strawberries, sugar and vanilla extract into a saucepan and ask an adult to bring the mixture to a simmer. Simmer for 5–8 minutes, or until the strawberries start to break down. Set the mixture aside to cool slightly.

5 Once the filling has cooled slightly, spoon it into the centre of each pastry case.

6 Roll out the remaining shortcrust pastry to 1/2 cm (1/4 in.) and cut into thin strips. Criss-cross the strips on top of each tart.

7 Ask an adult to put the tarts in the oven and bake for 10–12 minutes, or until the pastry is golden-brown. Remove the tarts from the oven and put them on a wire rack to cool.

8 Once cool, garnish with mint leaves and enjoy!

CREAM SANDWICHES

MAKES 8–10

Extra equipment:
- baking tray
- sieve
- ice cream scoop (optional)

Ingredients:
- 125 g (4 ½ oz) butter
- 100 g (4 oz) caster sugar
- 75 g (3 oz) brown sugar
- 1 egg
- a few drops of vanilla extract
- 150 g (5 oz) plain flour
- ½ teaspoon baking powder
- 50 g (2 oz) chocolate chips
- vanilla ice cream (see page 30 for homemade or use shop-bought)

1 Preheat the oven to 180°C / 350°F / gas mark 4.

2 Use a paper towel to grease the baking tray with a little butter.

3 Put the butter and both sugars in a large bowl and mix them together with a wooden spoon until they are pale, light and fluffy.

4 Add the egg and the vanilla extract and beat well.

5 Sift the flour and baking powder into the bowl. Stir them into the mixture and then add the chocolate chips.

6 Put 8–10 teaspoons of the mixture onto the baking tray – you will probably have enough mixture for two batches. Leave enough room between the cookies for them to expand while cooking. Bake the cookies for 15–20 minutes, or until golden brown.

7 Leave the cookies to cool for 2–3 minutes before lifting them onto a wire rack to cool completely.

8 Once the cookies are cool, take a scoop of ice cream and place it on top of a cookie, then sandwich another cookie on top. Eat immediately.

CHOCOLATE BANANAS

Extra equipment:
- tin foil
- baking tray

Ingredients:
- 8 bananas, skin on
- 100 g (4 oz) dark chocolate

1 Preheat the oven to 200°C / 400°F / gas mark 6.

2 Ask an adult to carefully slit each banana lengthways down the centre and through the skin, cutting about halfway through the banana.

3 Break the chocolate into small pieces and place a few pieces into the slit in each banana.

4 Wrap each banana in tin foil and then place onto the baking tray.

5 Place the bananas into the oven and bake for 10–15 minutes, just enough time to allow the bananas to heat and the chocolate to melt.

6 Ask an adult to remove the bananas from the oven, unwrap and enjoy!

TOP TIP!
Serve the bananas with squirty cream for an indulgent treat!

CARAMEL SHORTCAKE

MAKES 12

Extra equipment:
- 20 x 33 cm (8 x 13 in.) Swiss roll tin

Ingredients:
- 225 g (8 oz) plain flour
- 100 g (3 ½ oz) caster sugar
- 225 g (8 oz) butter, softened
- 100 g (3 ½ oz) semolina

For the topping:
- 175 g (6 oz) butter
- 175 g (6 oz) caster sugar
- 4 tablespoons golden syrup
- 400 g (14 oz) sweetened condensed milk
- 200 g (7 oz) plain chocolate, broken into pieces

1 Preheat the oven to 160°C / 320°F / gas mark 2. Grease the tin with a little butter.

2 Place the flour, caster sugar, butter and semolina into a bowl and mix together until it forms a smooth dough.

3 Press the mixture into the base of the Swiss roll tin, pushing it into all of the corners. Prick the dough with a fork and then bake in the oven for about 30–40 minutes until golden and firm. Leave to cool.

4 For the topping, ask an adult to put the butter, caster sugar, syrup and condensed milk into a saucepan and stir over a low heat until the butter has melted.

5 Stir the bubbling mixture for 5–8 minutes, stirring all of the time, until the mixture thickens.

6 Pour the mixture over the cooled shortbread and spread evenly over the base. Leave to cool.

7 Ask an adult to melt the chocolate in a heatproof bowl over a pan of simmering water, making sure the bowl doesn't touch the water. Pour the melted chocolate over the caramel mixture and then leave to cool.

8 Once cool, remove from the tin and cut into pieces.

CARAMEL NUT SWEETS

Extra equipment:

• sweet cases

Ingredients:

• 50 g (1 3/4 oz) granulated sugar

• 50 g (1 3/4 oz) brown sugar

• 85 ml (3 fl.oz) golden syrup

• 55 g (2 oz) butter

• 120 ml (4 fl.oz) double cream

• 1/2 teaspoon vanilla extract

• mixed nuts, to decorate

• dried fruit, to decorate

1 Ask an adult to put both sugars, golden syrup, butter and half of the cream into a saucepan. Bring the mixture to the boil, stirring often and then stir in the rest of the cream.

2 Heat without stirring until the mixture begins to change colour. When the mixture is ready you should be able to drop a small amount into cold water and it will form a firm ball (ask an adult to do this using a teaspoon).

3 Remove the mixture from the heat and stir in the vanilla extract.

4 Allow the mixture to cool a little, then spoon into the sweet cases.

5 Place a few mixed nuts and some dried fruit on top of each sweet to finish.

6 Place in the refrigerator to set.

39

BRAZILIAN BRIGADEIRO

MAKES 15-20

Extra equipment:
- baking tin
- mini paper cases

Ingredients:
- 200 g (7 oz) sweetened condensed milk
- 1/2 tablespoon butter
- 1 1/2 tablespoons cocoa powder
- 1/2 teaspoon vanilla extract
- dark chocolate sprinkles, to cover

1 Ask an adult to put the condensed milk, butter and cocoa powder into a saucepan over a medium heat.

2 Stir the mixture constantly, until it thickens enough to show the bottom of the pan when stirring, after about 10 minutes.

3 Remove the mixture from the heat and stir in the vanilla extract.

4 Grease the baking tin with butter and ask an adult to pour the mixture into the tin. Let the mixture cool to room temperature.

5 Grease your hands with a little butter and then take teaspoonfuls of the mixture and roll into small balls.

6 Roll each ball in the chocolate sprinkles until completely covered.

7 Place in mini paper cases and enjoy!

TOP TIP!
If the balls don't hold their shape, cook for another 5 minutes until the mixture thickens further.

HOT CROSS BUNS

Extra equipment:
- sieve
- damp cloth
- baking tray
- baking paper

Ingredients:
- 450 g (1 lb) white bread flour
- 7 g (1/2 oz) dried yeast
- 2 teaspoons ground cinnamon
- 1 teaspoon allspice
- 100 g (3 1/2 oz) dried fruit
- 1 orange, zest only
- 100 g (3 1/2 oz) sugar
- 50 g (1 1/2 oz) butter
- 250 ml (9 fl.oz) milk
- 1 egg

For the glaze:
- 1 egg, beaten

For the cross:
- 120 g (4 oz) icing sugar
- 1–2 tablespoons water

1 Sift the flour, dried yeast, cinnamon and allspice into a bowl and add the dried fruit, orange zest and sugar.

2 Place the butter and milk in a saucepan and warm until the butter has melted. Remove from the heat and mix in the egg. Fold the milk mixture into the flour mixture to make a dough.

3 Put the dough on a lightly floured surface and knead for 10 minutes or until the dough is smooth and elastic.

4 Split the dough into 12 pieces and shape into balls. Cover with a damp cloth and set aside for 1–2 hours, or until the dough has doubled in size.

5 Preheat the oven to 180°C / 350°F / gas mark 4. Line the baking tray with baking paper.

6 Place the buns onto the baking tray and brush with the beaten egg. Ask an adult to place in the oven and bake for 20–25 minutes, or until cooked through. Remove the buns from the oven, and leave to cool.

7 For the cross, mix the icing sugar with a little water until it forms a smooth icing. Use a teaspoon to drizzle the icing in a cross over each bun.

PUMPKIN MUFFINS

Extra equipment:
- muffin baking tray

Ingredients:
- 120 g (4 oz) prunes, puréed
- 165 g (6 oz) brown sugar
- 100 g (4 oz) golden syrup
- 245 g (9 oz) pumpkin flesh, puréed
- 2 egg whites
- 170 g (6 oz) plain flour
- 50 g (2 oz) polenta
- 1 teaspoon cinnamon
- 1 teaspoon nutmeg
- 1 teaspoon bicarbonate of soda

1 Preheat the oven to 200°C / 400°F / gas mark 6.

2 Use a paper towel to grease the muffin tray with a little soft butter.

3 In a large bowl mix together the prune purée, brown sugar, golden syrup, pumpkin and egg whites. Stir with a wooden spoon until they are well mixed.

4 In another bowl, mix together the flour, polenta, cinnamon, nutmeg and bicarbonate of soda.

5 Add the wet ingredients to the flour mixture. Use a tablespoon to gently mix the ingredients together.

6 Use a teaspoon to divide the mixture equally into the muffin tray. Bake the muffins for 20–25 minutes, or until golden brown.

7 Leave the muffins to cool in the tray, then remove.

TOP TIP!
These muffins are a great way to use up pumpkin flesh at Halloween.

WELSH CAKES

Extra equipment:
- sieve
- rolling pin
- 10 cm (4 in.) round cookie cutter
- heavy-based griddle or frying pan

Ingredients:
- 225 g (8 oz) self-raising flour
- 110 g (4 oz) salted butter, softened
- 85 g (3 oz) caster sugar
- handful of sultanas
- 1 egg
- milk, if needed
- extra butter, for greasing
- extra caster sugar, for dusting

1 Sieve the flour into a bowl and add the butter. Use your hands to mix the butter into the flour until the mixture resembles breadcrumbs.

2 Mix in the sugar, sultanas and egg until it forms a ball of dough. Add a splash of milk if the mixture is too dry.

3 Roll out the mixture until it is about 1/2 cm (1/4 in.) thick. Then, use the cookie cutter to cut out circles of dough.

4 Ask an adult to grease the griddle or frying pan with a little butter and place on the heat.

5 Once hot, place the Welsh cakes on the griddle, turning once. Each Welsh cake should take about 2–3 minutes per side – it should be caramel brown before turning.

6 Remove from the pan and dust with caster sugar while still warm.

TOP TIP!
Replace the sultanas with chocolate chips for a chocolatey treat.

HOMEMADE JAFFA CAKES

Extra equipment:
- cupcake tray
- shallow-sided baking tray
- small round cookie cutter

Ingredients:
- 2 eggs
- 50 g (2 oz) caster sugar
- 50 g (2 oz) plain flour, sieved

For the filling:
- 135 g (5 oz) packet orange jelly, chopped
- 1 tablespoon orange marmalade
- 125 ml (4 1/2 fl.oz) boiling water

For the topping:
- 200 g (7 oz) dark chocolate, broken into pieces

1 Preheat the oven to 180°C / 350°F / gas mark 4.

2 Ask an adult to place a heatproof bowl over a saucepan of simmering water, making sure the base of the bowl doesn't touch the water. Put the eggs and sugar in the bowl and stir continuously for 4–5 minutes, or until the mixture is pale, fluffy and well combined. Add the flour, still stirring continuously, until a thick, smooth batter forms.

3 Half-fill each space in the cupcake tray with the mixture. Ask an adult to put the tray in the oven and bake for 8–10 minutes, or until pale golden-brown and cooked through. Remove from the oven and leave to cool in the tray.

4 Then, ask an adult to mix together the jelly, marmalade and boiling water until the jelly has dissolved and the mixture is smooth. Pour the mixture into the baking tray to form a 1 cm (1/2 in.) layer of jelly. Leave to cool completely, then put the jelly in the refrigerator to set.

5 Cut small circles from the jelly using a cookie cutter slightly smaller than the cake bases. Put a jelly disc on top of each cake.

6 Ask an adult to place a heatproof bowl over a saucepan of simmering water, making sure the base of the bowl doesn't touch the water. Add the chocolate and stir until melted and glossy then pour over the cakes. Leave the chocolate to cool and set.

FRUITY LOLLIES

Extra equipment:
• blender
• ice lolly moulds

Ingredients:
• 220 g (7 ¾ oz) pineapple
• 2 very ripe bananas
• 2 tablespoons clear honey
• 500 ml (16 fl.oz) plain yogurt

1 Ask an adult to carefully cut up the pineapple into small chunks. Then, cut up the bananas into slices.

2 Place the pineapple, banana, honey and yogurt into a blender and blend until smooth. If you have not got a blender, place the ingredients into a bowl and ask an adult to blend the mixture with a hand-held electric whisk.

3 Pour the mixture into the ice lolly moulds and place in the freezer. Leave them to set for at least 4 hours, until solid.

4 Remove the ice lollies from the freezer and let them stand at room temperature for 5 minutes. Then, remove from the moulds and enjoy!

TOP TIP!
Any leftover mixture can be made into a smoothie! Just blitz it in a blender with some more yogurt and milk if it is too thick!

CINNAMON BUNS

Extra equipment:
- cling film • food processor
- rolling pin
- two 20 x 30 cm (8 x 12 in.) deep baking trays

Ingredients:
- 450 g (16 oz) strong white flour
- 50 g (1 ³/4 oz) caster sugar
- 1 teaspoon salt
- 85 g (3 oz) butter
- 7 g (¹/4 oz) dried yeast
- 2 eggs, beaten
- 150 ml (5 fl.oz) milk
- 2 teaspoons ground cinnamon
- 85 g (3 oz) light brown sugar
- 100 g (3 ¹/2 oz) pecans
- 125 g (4 ¹/2 oz) butter, melted

For the topping:
- 125 ml (4 ¹/4 fl.oz) maple syrup
- 50 g (1 ³/4 oz) light brown sugar
- 100 g (3 ¹/2 oz) pecans, chopped

1 Put the flour, sugar, salt and butter into a bowl and use your fingers to rub the butter in until the mixture becomes crumbly. Add the yeast, eggs and milk and mix well to form a soft dough. Knead for about 15 minutes, or until the dough is smooth and springy. Place the dough in a lightly oiled bowl, cover with cling film and leave to rise for about an hour, or until doubled in size.

2 Ask an adult to put the cinnamon, sugar and pecans into a food processor and pulse until the nuts are finely ground.

3 Divide the dough into two. Roll out each half on a lightly floured work surface to make two 25 x 35 cm (10 x 14 in.) rectangles.

4 Brush each rectangle with a little melted butter. Then, spread half of the pecan mixture over each dough, pressing it down. With the long end of the rectangle in front of you, tightly roll up the dough and pinch the edges together to seal. Cut each dough into five equal pieces.

5 Mix the maple syrup, brown sugar, remaining melted butter and chopped pecans together, then pour equally into the two baking trays. Place the buns onto the baking trays. Cover with lightly oiled cling film and put in a warm place for about 30 minutes. Preheat the oven to 180°C / 350°F / gas mark 4. Remove the cling film and bake the cinnamon buns in the oven for 30 minutes, or until lightly browned.

BANANA WALNUT MUFFINS

MAKES 12

Extra equipment:
• muffin baking tray

Ingredients:
• 3 ripe bananas
• 100 g (4 oz) caster sugar
• 70 g (2 oz) brown sugar
• 2 eggs
• 100 g (4 oz) butter, melted
• 1 ½ teaspoons bicarbonate
  of soda
• 110 g (4 oz) plain flour
• 110 g (4 oz) wholemeal flour
• 45 ml (1 ½ fl.oz) buttermilk
• 145 g (5 oz) walnuts, chopped

1 Preheat the oven to 180°C / 350°F / gas mark 4.

2 Use a paper towel to grease the muffin tray with a little soft butter.

3 Mash the bananas in a mixing bowl.

4 Add the caster sugar, brown sugar and eggs and stir together until well mixed.

5 Add the melted butter and mix. Sift in the bicarbonate of soda and plain flour, and then add the wholemeal flour, mixing well.

6 Add the buttermilk and walnuts. Stir the mixture until well combined.

7 Use a teaspoon to divide the mixture equally into the muffin tray. Bake the muffins for 20 minutes, or until golden brown.

8 Leave the muffins in the tray until they are cool, and then turn out and enjoy.

DOUGHNUTS

Extra equipment:
- sieve
- rolling pin
- piping bag
- card heart-shaped cut-outs

Ingredients:
- 2 eggs
- 100 g (3 ½ oz) caster sugar
- 1 vanilla pod, seeds scraped out
- 100 ml (3 ½ fl.oz) crème fraîche
- 375 g (13 ½ oz) plain flour, plus extra for dusting
- pinch of salt
- 1 tablespoon baking powder
- 1 teaspoon bicarbonate of soda
- vegetable oil, for deep frying
- custard or jam, softened
- icing sugar, to dust

1 In a bowl, beat the eggs, sugar and vanilla seeds for 5 minutes, then stir in the crème fraîche.

2 Sift in the flour, salt, baking powder and bicarbonate of soda and mix well. Knead on a floured surface for 2–3 minutes until the dough is smooth.

3 Roll out the dough to about ½ cm (¼ in.) thick and cut out 7 ½ cm (3 in.) circles.

4 Ask an adult to half-fill a large saucepan with vegetable oil and heat until a small cube of bread turns golden in 30 seconds. **Do not leave hot oil unattended.**

5 Ask an adult to fry the doughnuts in the oil for 3–4 minutes, or until golden-brown. Do this in batches to avoid over-crowding the pan.

6 Place the softened custard or jam into the piping bag. Once the doughnuts have cooled slightly, pipe in the custard or jam.

7 Hold the card heart-shaped cut-outs over the doughnuts and sprinkle with icing sugar to finish.

MACAROONS

Extra equipment:
- 2 baking trays
- baking paper
- food processor
- sieve
- whisk
- piping bag with 1 cm (1/2 in.) plain nozzle

Ingredients:
- 175 g (6 oz) icing sugar
- 125 g (4 1/2 oz) ground almonds
- 3 egg whites
- pinch of salt
- 75 g (2 1/2 oz) caster sugar
- food colouring

For the filling:
- 150 g (5 1/4 oz) butter, softened
- 75 g (2 1/2 oz) icing sugar
- food colouring (optional)

1 Preheat the oven to 160°C / 320°F / gas mark 3. Line both baking trays with baking paper.

2 Place the icing sugar and ground almonds in a food processor and blend to a very fine mixture, then sift into a bowl.

3 In a separate bowl, whisk the egg whites with a pinch of salt to soft peaks, then gradually whisk in the caster sugar until the mixture is thick and glossy. Add a few drops of food colouring. If you want, separate the mixture into batches and colour each individually.

4 Fold half the almond and icing sugar mixture into the meringue and mix well. Add the remaining half, mixing until it is shiny and thick.

5 Spoon the mixture into a piping bag fitted with a 1 cm (1/2 in.) plain nozzle. Pipe small rounds of the macaroon mixture, about 3 cm (1 in.) across, onto the baking trays.

6 Leave the macaroons to stand at room temperature for 10–15 minutes to form a slight skin. Place in the oven and bake for 15 minutes. Remove from the oven and cool.

7 For the filling, beat the butter until light and fluffy, then beat in the icing sugar. Add a few drops of food colouring to match the macaroons (optional).

8 Spread the filling onto the cooled macaroons and sandwich together.

49

SWEDISH CHOCOLATE BALLS

MAKES 15-20

Ingredients:
- 100 g (3 1/2 oz) rolled oats
- 80 g (3 oz) caster sugar
- 15 g (1/2 oz) cocoa powder
- 70 g (2 1/2 oz) butter, softened
- 20 g (3/4 oz) unsweetened baking chocolate
- 1–2 teaspoons strong coffee
- 1/4 teaspoon vanilla extract
- desiccated coconut, to decorate

1 Mix the oats, sugar and cocoa powder in a bowl. Add the butter and mix to form a thick dough.

2 Ask an adult to place a heatproof bowl over a saucepan of simmering water, making sure the base doesn't touch the water. Melt the chocolate, then stir the coffee, vanilla extract and melted chocolate into the oats mixture until well combined.

3 Put the desiccated coconut into a small bowl.

4 Take small amounts of the chocolate mixture and roll them in your hands to form small balls about 4 cm (1 1/2 in.) in diameter.

5 Roll the balls in the desiccated coconut until completely covered.

6 Place the balls in the refrigerator for 1–2 hours to firm slightly, then enjoy!

BLUEBERRY MUFFINS

Extra equipment:
- paper cases
- muffin baking tray

Ingredients:
- 55 g (2 oz) butter
- 2 eggs
- 200 g (7 oz) sugar
- 250 g (9 oz) plain flour
- 2 teaspoons baking powder
- 110 ml (4 fl.oz) milk
- 1 teaspoon vanilla essence
- 290 g (10 oz) blueberries

For the topping:
- 120 g (4 oz) icing sugar
- 1–2 tablespoons water

1. Preheat the oven to 180°C / 350°F / gas mark 4. Place the paper cases in the muffin tray.

2. Place the butter, eggs and sugar into a large bowl and beat until well mixed.

3. Mix the flour with the baking powder and sift into the butter mixture, alternating with the milk.

4. Mix in the vanilla essence, then add the blueberries. Stir everything together until just moistened.

5. Use a teaspoon to divide the mixture equally into the paper cases. Bake the muffins for 30 minutes, or until golden brown.

6. Once cooked, ask an adult to remove the muffins from the oven and cool on a wire rack.

7. For the icing, place the icing sugar into a bowl with the water. Mix together to form a smooth icing.

8. While the muffins are still warm, spoon a little of the icing over each one. Leave to cool completely.

TOP TIP!
Experiment with other berries – try raspberries or blackberries!

MAKES 16

Extra equipment:
• 20 cm (8 in.) square cake tin

Ingredients:
• 225 g (8 oz) caster sugar
• 4 eggs
• 225 g (8 oz) butter, melted
• 150 g (5 ½ oz) plain flour, sieved
• 225 g (8 oz) white chocolate, chopped
• 100 g (3 ½ oz) pecan nuts, chopped

1 Preheat the oven to 180°C / 350°F / gas mark 4.

2 Grease the cake tin with a little butter.

3 Beat together the sugar and eggs until pale and fluffy. Beat in the melted butter a little at a time, making sure it is well mixed.

4 Using a metal spoon, carefully fold in the flour. Then, add the chopped white chocolate and pecan nuts, carefully mixing in a little at a time.

5 Spoon the blondie mix into the cake tin and smooth out the top.

6 Ask an adult to place in the oven and bake for 30–35 minutes, or until a skewer inserted into the centre comes out clean.

7 Leave to cool completely.

8 Once cool, remove from the tin and cut into squares.

TOP TIP!
Try icing the blondies with vanilla buttercream mixed with some peanut butter.

SCOTCH PANCAKES

Extra equipment:
- whisk

Ingredients:
- 110 g (4 oz) plain flour
- 1/2 teaspoon bicarbonate of soda
- 1 egg
- 1 tablespoon vegetable oil
- 1 tablespoon golden syrup
- 150 ml (5 fl.oz) milk

To serve:
- fresh fruit (optional)
- golden syrup (optional)

1 Put the flour and bicarbonate of soda into a bowl.

2 In a separate bowl, mix the egg, oil and golden syrup and whisk together. Add the milk and mix well.

3 Pour the milk mixture into the dry ingredients and whisk thoroughly to form a batter.

4 Ask an adult to heat a non-stick frying pan. Pour in 1 1/2 tablespoons of the batter for each pancake.

5 When bubbles appear in the batter of the pancake, flip it over and cook until golden brown on both sides.

6 Cook the remaining batter and then serve warm, topped with fresh fruit and more golden syrup!

BAKLAVA

TOP TIP! Many baklava recipes use rose water or orange-flower water to flavour the syrup.

Extra equipment:
- 23 cm (9 in.) square baking dish
- baking paper
- food processor

Ingredients:
- 300 g (10 ½ oz) pistachios, plus extra to serve
- 3 limes, zest only
- 75 g (2 ½ oz) caster sugar
- 2 tablespoons poppy seeds
- pinch ground cloves
- 400 g (14 oz) ready-made filo pastry
- 225 g (8 oz) butter, melted

For the syrup:
- 175 g (6 oz) honey
- 125 g (4 ½ oz) caster sugar
- 3 limes, juice only
- 250 ml (8 ½ fl.oz) water

1 Preheat the oven to 150°C / 300°F / gas mark 2. Grease and line the baking dish.

2 Ask an adult to put the pistachios, lime zest, sugar, poppy seeds and cloves into a food processor and pulse until the mixture resembles breadcrumbs.

3 Cut the filo pastry so it fits inside the baking dish. Put a sheet of pastry into the dish and brush with melted butter. Repeat this process until you have six layers of pastry.

4 Spread a third of the pistachio mixture over the pastry then cover with another layer of pastry, buttering each piece.

5 Repeat this process twice more, using the remaining two-thirds of the pistachio mixture, and then top with a final layer of pastry.

6 Put the baklava in the oven for an hour, or until crisp and golden-brown on top.

7 Ask an adult to heat the honey, sugar, lime juice and water in a saucepan over a medium heat. Cook until the sugar has melted and a syrup has formed, after about 20 minutes.

8 Ask an adult to pour the syrup over the filo pastry and then leave to cool completely. Once cool, cut the baklava into slices and serve with a sprinkling of finely chopped or grated pistachios.

LADYBIRD BISCUITS

Extra equipment:
- baking tray
- baking paper
- sieve
- rolling pin
- round cookie cutter
- palette knife

Ingredients:
- 100 g (4 oz) butter
- 100 g (4 oz) caster sugar
- 1 egg
- 1 teaspoon vanilla extract
- 275 g (10 oz) plain flour

For the icing:
- 400 g (14 oz) icing sugar
- 3–4 tablespoons water
- red food colouring
- dark chocolate, melted

1 Preheat the oven to 190°C / 375°F / gas mark 5. Line the baking tray with baking paper.

2 Cream the butter and sugar together in a bowl until light and fluffy. Add the egg and vanilla extract, a little at a time, and mix well.

3 Sift the flour into the creamed mixture and, using your hands, create a smooth, firm dough. Refrigerate the mixture for 15 minutes.

4 Roll the dough out on a floured surface until it is 1 cm (1/2 in.) thick. Using the cookie cutter, cut the dough into circles and transfer to the baking tray.

5 Bake the biscuits in the oven for 8–10 minutes, or until golden brown, and then transfer to a wire rack to cool.

6 To make the icing, sift the icing sugar into a bowl and add enough water to make a smooth, thick paste. Add one or two drops of red food colouring to three-quarters of the icing, reserving some white for later. With the palette knife, spread the red icing over each biscuit and leave to set.

7 Use the melted dark chocolate to decorate each biscuit with spots and a head and leave to set. To finish, use the reserved white icing for the eyes, topping them off with chocolate for the pupils.

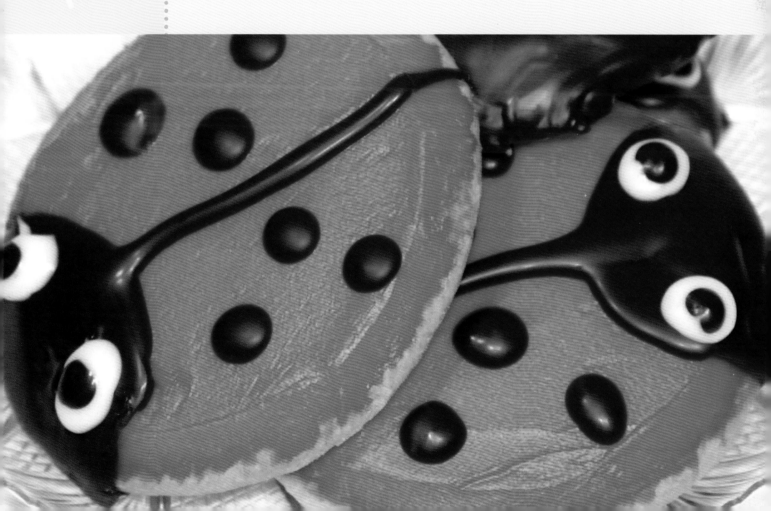

SHORTBREAD

MAKES 8

Extra equipment:
- sieve
- 20 cm (8 in.) loose-bottomed round cake tin

Ingredients:
- 130 g (4 1/2 oz) butter, softened
- 60 g (2 1/2 oz) caster sugar, plus extra for sprinkling
- 130 g (4 1/2 oz) plain flour
- 60 g (2 1/2 oz) rice flour
- pinch of salt

1 Preheat the oven to 170°C / 325°F / gas mark 3.

2 Cream the butter and sugar together in a large bowl, until pale and fluffy.

3 Sift in both flours and the salt and mix well.

4 Use your hands to bring the mixture together and press it into the cake tin. Smooth the top with the back of a spoon. Score the mixture into eight pieces with a knife and prick each piece with a fork. Use your thumb to indent around the edge of the shortbread.

5 Put the mixture in the refrigerator for 30 minutes to firm.

6 Remove the shortbread from the refrigerator and bake for 30–35 minutes, or until pale golden-brown.

7 Ask an adult to remove the shortbread from the oven and sprinkle with a little caster sugar.

8 Leave the shortbread to cool in the tin for a few minutes. Then, remove it from the tin and leave to cool completely on a wire rack.

9 Cut the shortbread into eight pieces, along the scored lines, and enjoy!

CRISPY CAKES

Extra equipment:
- paper cases

Ingredients:
- 50 g (2 oz) butter
- 1 teaspoon vanilla extract
- 200 g (7 oz) marshmallows
- 100 g (4 oz) crisped rice cereal

1 In a large saucepan, ask an adult to melt the butter over a low heat.

2 Add the vanilla extract, and then melt the marshmallows into the butter, stirring continuously.

3 When the marshmallows have melted, add the cereal and mix until it is evenly coated.

4 Allow the mixture to cool slightly, then spoon the mixture into paper cases.

5 Leave the crispy cakes for 2–3 hours to set completely and then enjoy!

TOP TIP! Why not add sweets or chocolate chips along with the crisped cereal?

SCONES

MAKES 8-10

Extra equipment:

- baking tray
- sieve
- rolling pin
- 5 cm (2 in.) round pastry cutter

Ingredients:

- 225 g (8 oz) self-raising flour
- 1 teaspoon baking powder
- pinch of salt
- 25 g (1 oz) caster sugar
- 50 g (2 oz) unsalted butter, softened
- 150 ml (5 fl.oz) milk
- 1 egg, beaten
- clotted cream, to serve
- jam, to serve

1 Preheat the oven to 220°C / 425°F / gas mark 7. Grease the baking tray with a little butter.

2 Sift together the flour, baking powder and salt into a bowl. Stir in the sugar.

3 Add the butter and rub it into the flour mixture until it resembles fine breadcrumbs.

4 Add the milk, a little at a time, until it becomes a smooth dough.

5 Lightly flour the work surface and then roll out the dough until it is about 2 cm (³/4 in.) thick.

6 Use the pastry cutter to cut the dough into round scones. Re-roll any dough that is left over and cut out more scones. Place onto the baking tray.

7 Brush the tops of the scones with the beaten egg. Ask an adult to place in the oven and bake for 10–12 minutes, or until golden brown.

8 Serve with clotted cream and jam.

TOP TIP!
Why not try making fruit scones by adding 50 g (2 oz) raisins or sultanas to the dry ingredients?

FRUIT SALAD SUNDAES

Extra equipment:

- cling film
- ice cream scoop (optional)
- four sundae glasses

Ingredients:

- 2 green apples
- 200 g (7 oz) fresh pineapple
- 200 g (7 oz) strawberries
- 100 g (3 1/2 oz) red and green seedless grapes
- 75 ml (2 1/2 fl.oz) fresh fruit juice
- vanilla ice cream (see recipe on page 30 for homemade or use shop-bought)

To decorate:

- whipped cream
- assorted sweets
- strawberry sauce
- 4 cone wafers

1 Ask an adult to core each apple and cut it into thin slices. Then, cut the pineapple into small chunks and slice the strawberries.

2 Put the apple, pineapple, strawberries and grapes into a bowl and pour over the fruit juice. Cover with cling film and leave to chill in the refrigerator for at least 30 minutes.

3 Take a scoop of vanilla ice cream and place at the bottom of each sundae glass. Then, spoon over some of the fruit mixture.

4 Continue layering the ice cream and fruit salad until each sundae glass is nearly full.

5 To finish, top each sundae with some whipped cream. Sprinkle with your favourite sweets, a drizzle of strawberry sauce and a cone wafer. Eat immediately.

TOP TIP!
Experiment with the fruits – try using fruit in season.

59

CREAM BON BONS

Extra equipment:
• baking tray
• greaseproof paper
• melon baller (optional)

Ingredients:
• 500 ml (17 fl.oz) vanilla ice cream (see recipe on page 30 for homemade or use shop-bought)
• 200 g (7 oz) dark chocolate
• 100 g (3 1/2 oz) almonds, chopped

1 Cover the baking tray with greaseproof paper.

2 Scoop the ice cream into small, round balls. Use a melon baller if you have one.

3 Place the ice cream balls onto the baking tray and then place in the freezer for an hour.

4 Ask an adult to put a heatproof bowl over a saucepan of just simmering water, making sure the bowl doesn't touch the water. Break the chocolate into small pieces and put them in the bowl.

5 Stir until the chocolate has melted and then mix in the almonds thoroughly.

6 Take the chocolate off the heat and allow to cool to just before it stiffens again.

7 Dip each ice cream ball into the cooled chocolate mixture.

8 Return to the baking tray and place back in the freezer to set the chocolate.

TOP TIP!
Experiment with the ice cream flavour, chocolate and nuts until you find your perfect combination!

RASPBERRY SEMIFREDDO

Extra equipment:
- 1 kg (2 lb) loaf tin
- baking paper
- whisk
- cling film
- tin foil
- sieve (if making a coulis)

Ingredients:
- 100 g (3 1/2 oz) fresh or frozen (thawed) raspberries
- 85 g (3 oz) golden caster sugar
- 280 ml (9 1/2 fl.oz) double cream
- 400 ml (13 1/2 fl.oz) crème fraîche
- 50 g (1 3/4 oz) pistachios, chopped

1 Line the base of the loaf tin with baking paper.

2 Place the raspberries and half of the sugar together in a bowl and mix with a fork, leaving some raspberries whole.

3 Whisk the cream together with the rest of the sugar, until it holds soft peaks.

4 Beat the crème fraîche until it holds soft peaks like the cream, then gently fold it into the cream mixture.

5 Fold the raspberry mixture and chopped pistachios into the cream and stir it a few times – just enough to swirl them through the mixture. Pour the mixture into the loaf tin and gently smooth the top.

6 Place the semifreddo in the freezer until just firm, then cover with cling film and tin foil until ready to be eaten.

7 When ready to serve, take the semifreddo out of the freezer and place in the refrigerator for about an hour. Remove from the loaf tin and cut into slices. Scatter some fresh raspberries on top and enjoy!

TOP TIP!
Make a raspberry coulis to serve with the semifreddo by mashing 100 g (3 1/2 oz) raspberries with one tablespoon icing sugar, and then pressing through a sieve.

DATE MUFFINS

Extra equipment:
- muffin baking tray
- paper cases

Ingredients:
- 225 g (8 oz) plain flour
- 1 tablespoon baking powder
- ½ teaspoon bicarbonate of soda
- 75 g (2 ½ oz) demerara sugar
- 1 teaspoon cinnamon
- zest of 1 small orange
- 150 ml (5 fl.oz) milk
- 1 egg
- 50 g (1 ¾ oz) butter, melted
- 250 g (9 oz) pitted dates, chopped

1 Preheat the oven to 200°C / 400°F / gas mark 6. Line the muffin tray with paper cases.

2 Mix together the flour, baking powder, bicarbonate of soda, sugar, cinnamon and orange zest.

3 In a separate bowl, mix the milk, egg and melted butter. Add to the flour mixture and fold together until just mixed.

4 Then, stir in the chopped dates, reserving a few to top each muffin.

5 Divide the mixture into the paper cases and place some of the reserved chopped dates on top.

6 Ask an adult to place the muffins in the oven and cook for 15–20 minutes, or until just risen and firm. Transfer to a wire rack to cool.

TOP TIP!
Why not add your favourite seeds or nuts in step 4!

CHOCOLATE CROISSANTS

Extra equipment:
• baking tray
• baking paper

Ingredients:
• 375 g (13 oz) ready-rolled butter puff pastry
• 100 g (3 ½ oz) dark, or good-quality milk, chocolate
• 1 egg, beaten

1 Preheat the oven to 220°C / 430°F / gas mark 7.

2 Line the baking tray with baking paper.

3 Unroll the puff pastry and cut it into six equal squares. Cut each square in half to form two rectangles.

4 Break the chocolate into 1 cm (½ in.) pieces. Place a couple of pieces of chocolate on each rectangle about 2 cm (¾ in.) above the bottom.

5 Roll each rectangle up lengthways. Seal it by squeezing the edges together with your finger.

6 Put the croissants onto the baking tray and brush with the beaten egg.

7 Ask an adult to place in the oven for 15 minutes, or until they are golden and puffy.

TOP TIP!
Experiment with the fillings – try flavoured jams or spreads.

63

INDEX OF RECIPES

Baklava	54	Ice Cream Bon Bons	60
Banana Walnut Muffins	47	Ice Cream Cones	30
Blondies	52	Ice Cream Sandwiches	36
Blueberry Muffins	51	Iced Biscuits	23
Brazilian Brigadeiro	40	Indoor Smores	12
Caramel Apples	29	Ladybird Biscuits	55
Caramel Lollipops	20	Lemon Poppy Muffins	16
Caramel Nut Sweets	39	Liquorice Truffles	28
Caramel Shortcake	38	Macaroons	49
Chocolate Bananas	37	Mini Jammy Tarts	35
Chocolate Croissants	63	Nutty Nougat Parfait	14
Chocolate Drops	19	Peanut Brittle	25
Chocolate Fondant Fancies	33	Peanut Butter Cups	10
Chocolate Mice	11	Peppermint Creams	13
Chocolate Truffles	21	Pumpkin Muffins	42
Cinnamon Buns	46	Raspberry Semifreddo	61
Coconut Ice	18	Rock Candy	15
Colourful Meringues	32	Rocky Road	26
Crispy Cakes	57	Scones	58
Date Muffins	62	Scotch Pancakes	53
Doughnuts	48	Shortbread	56
Flourless Brownies	27	Sticky Toffee Popcorn	17
Fruit Salad Sundaes	59	Swedish Chocolate Balls	50
Fruity Lollies	45	Sweetie Cookies	31
Homemade Jaffa Cakes	44	Traffic Light Jelly	34
Honeycomb	22	Vanilla Fudge	24
Hot Cross Buns	41	Welsh Cakes	43

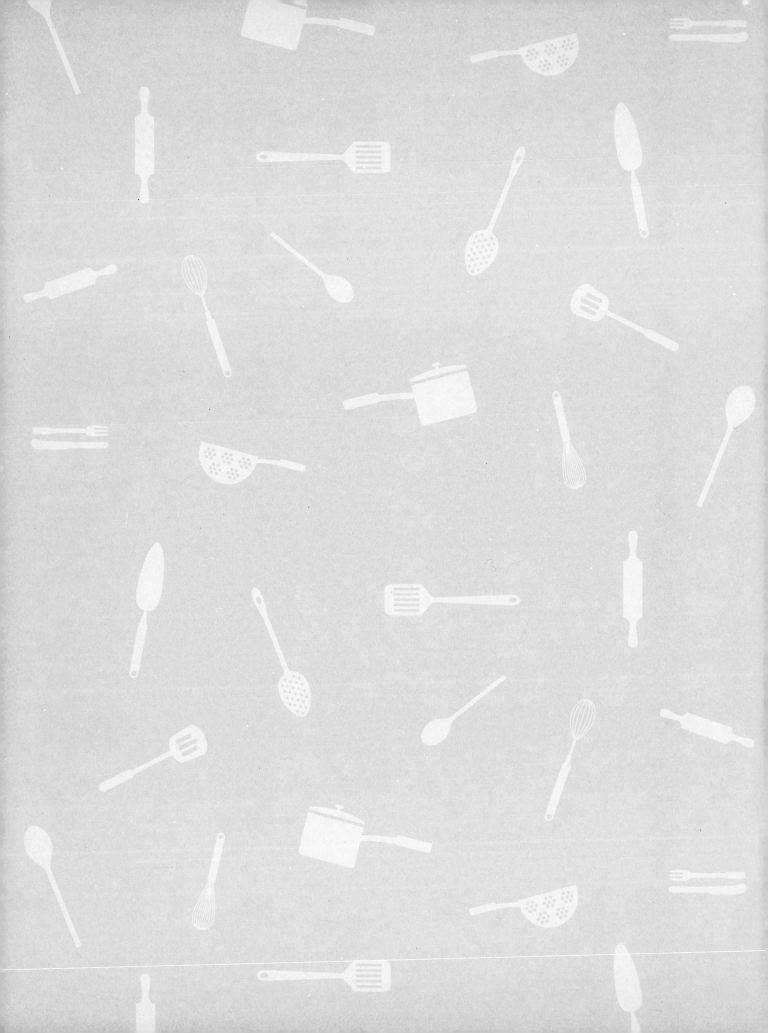